D1128130

ELEMENTS OF *Writing*

REVISED EDITION

WORD CHOICE

and

SENTENCE STYLE

WORKSHEETS
WITH ANSWER KEYS

▶ Fourth Course

HOLT, RINEHART AND WINSTON

Harcourt Brace & Company

Austin • *New York* • *Orlando* • *Atlanta* • *San Francisco* • *Boston* • *Dallas* • *Toronto* • *London*

Staff Credits

Associate Director: Mescal Evler

Managing Editor: Steve Welch

Project Editors: Susan Sims Britt, Susan Lynch

Editorial Staff: *Editors,* Jonathan David Carson, Adrienne Greer; *Copy Editors,* Joseph S. Schofield IV, Atietie O. Tonwe; *Coordinators,* Susan G. Alexander, Amanda F. Beard, Rebecca Bennett, Mark W. Holland, Wendy Langabeer, Marie Hoffman Price; *Support,* Ruth A. Hooker, Kelly Keeley, Margaret Sanchez, Pat Stover

Design: Christine Schueler

Editorial Permissions: Janet Harrington

Production Coordinator: Rosa Mayo Degollado

Electronic Publishing Supervisor: Barbara Hudgens

Electronic Publishing Staff: Heather Jernt, *Project Coordinator*
Rina May Ouellette, Michele Ruschhaupt, Charlie Taliaferro, Ethan Thompson

Contributing Writers

Judith Austin-Mills
Bill Martin
Matthew H. Pangborn
Raymond Teague

Copyright © by Holt, Rinehart and Winston, Inc.

All rights reserved. No part of this publication may be reproduced or transmitted in any form or by any means, electronic or mechanical, including photocopy, recording, or any information storage and retrieval system, without permission in writing from the publisher.

Permission is hereby granted to reproduce Blackline Masters in this publication in complete pages for instructional use and not for resale by any teacher using ELEMENTS OF WRITING.

Printed in the United States of America

ISBN 0-03-051182-8

1 2 3 4 5 085 00 99 98 97

Contents

To the Teacher

The teacher support provided by the *Annotated Teacher's Edition* is further reinforced by the *Teaching Resources*.

The *Teaching Resources* have been designed to help you in your classroom—where the demands on your time and energy are great—to deal with each student as an individual.

This booklet, *Word Choice and Sentence Style*, contains practice and reinforcement copying masters as well as Reviews (Forms A and B) covering material presented in Chapters 12–14 of the *Pupil's Edition*. Worksheets are organized by chapter, and answer keys are included at the end of each chapter.

Word Choice and Sentence Style is the third in a series of eight booklets comprising the *Teaching Resources*.

- *Practicing the Writing Process*
- *Strategies for Writing*
- **Word Choice and Sentence Style**
- *Language Skills Practice and Assessment*
- *Academic and Workplace Skills*
- *Holistic Scoring: Prompts and Models*
- *Portfolio Assessment*
- *Practice for Assessment in Reading, Vocabulary, and Spelling*

Chapter 12: Writing Complete Sentences

Types of Sentence Fragments A

A **sentence fragment** is a group of words that is only part of a sentence.

To find out whether you have a complete sentence or a sentence fragment, you can use a simple three-part test:

1. Does the group of words have a subject?
2. Does it have a verb?
3. Does it express a complete thought?

If even one of your answers is no, then you have a fragment.

Exercise A   For each of the following word groups that is a complete sentence, write **C**. If the word group is missing a subject, write **S**. If the word group is missing a verb, write **V**.

_____ 1. Harriet Quimby, a famous aviator.

_____ 2. Flew across the English Channel.

_____ 3. Louis Blériot, another famous navigator, lent her the plane.

_____ 4. She landed in France.

_____ 5. Died in a flying accident later that year.

_____ 6. Quimby, whose picture was on the cover of magazines.

_____ 7. Was a magazine writer and the first female pilot from the United States.

_____ 8. In France another female pilot.

_____ 9. Baroness Raymonde de la Roche.

_____ 10. De la Roche learned to fly in 1909.

Exercise B   On the lines provided, rewrite each sentence fragment as a complete sentence.

1. a deep faith in states' rights

_____

2. seceded from the Union

_____

3. protested the election of Abraham Lincoln

_____

4. Jefferson Davis, a mild-mannered man

_____

5. the issue of slavery

_____

Chapter 12: Writing Complete Sentences

Types of Sentence Fragments B

A **phrase** is a group of words that does not contain a subject and a verb. Three kinds of phrases are often mistaken for complete sentences: verbal phrases, appositive phrases, and prepositional phrases.

Verbals are forms of verbs that are used as other parts of speech. One type of verbal usually ends in -*ing*, -*d*, or -*ed* and doesn't have a helping verb. Another type of verbal has the word *to* in front of the verb. A **verbal phrase** is a phrase that contains a verbal.

> **Verbal phrases:** seeing the movie, built in 1900, to cook dinner
> **Complete sentence:** Mr. Wu started to cook dinner.

An appositive is a word that identifies or explains a nearby word in the sentence. An **appositive phrase**, a phrase made up of an appositive and its modifiers, is a fragment. It does not contain the basic parts of a sentence.

> **Appositive phrase:** a popular singer
> **Complete sentence:** Janet Jackson, a popular singer, appeared on stage.

A **prepositional phrase** is a group of words beginning with a preposition and ending with a noun or pronoun. A prepositional phrase can't stand alone as a sentence because it doesn't express a complete thought.

> **Prepositional phrase:** at sunset
> **Complete sentence:** We went home at sunset.

A **subordinate clause** fragment is easy to identify because it suggests a question that it doesn't answer.

> **Subordinate clause:** that I loved [*What* was loved?]
> **Complete sentence:** Here is the book that I loved.

Exercise A   For each of the following groups of words that is a verbal phrase, write **VP**, for each appositive phrase, write **AP**, for each prepositional phrase, write **PP**, and for each subordinate clause, write **SC.**

_____ 1. in Harlem

_____ 2. that are neglected

_____ 3. to move to lower Manhattan

_____ 4. a restored area

Exercise B   Create sentences from the following groups of words by attaching them to a complete sentence or by adding subjects and verbs as needed.

1. tasting the different breads

_____

2. at the West Indian takeout

_____

Chapter 12: Writing Complete Sentences

Identifying Run-on Sentences

There are two kinds of **run-on sentences:** the fused sentence and the comma splice. In a **fused sentence,** a writer joins two or more sentences with no punctuation between them.

> **Fused sentence:** I saw the film I liked it.
>
> **Correct:** I saw the film. I liked it.

In a **comma splice,** a writer joins two or more sentences with only a comma between them.

> **Comma splice:** Shira went to the temple, she found comfort there.
>
> **Correct:** Shira went to the temple. She found comfort there.

Here are three ways to revise run-on sentences:

1. You can make a compound sentence by adding a comma and a coordinating conjunction (such as *and, yet, but,* or *or*).

   Shira went to the temple, *and* she found comfort there.

2. You can make a compound sentence by adding a semicolon.

   Shira went to the temple; she found comfort there.

3. You can make a compound sentence by adding a semicolon and a conjunctive adverb, such as *therefore, instead, meanwhile, still, also, nevertheless,* or *however.* Follow a conjunctive adverb with a comma.

   Shira prayed often; *therefore,* she found comfort at the temple.

Exercise A   For each group of words that is a fused sentence, write **FS.** For each group of words that is a comma splice, write **CS.**

_____ 1. She attended the Saturday service her mother did, too.

_____ 2. The rabbi spoke about brotherly love, the congregation listened intently.

_____ 3. She read from the Torah Robin read also.

_____ 4. They read well, they pronounced the Hebrew correctly.

_____ 5. They attend a reformed temple women can be on the bema, or platform, in their temple.

Exercise B   Correct each of the following run-on sentences by using the method specified in parentheses.

1. I will hear the news on Saturday. Elmo will find out on Sunday. (Make a compound sentence using a comma and a coordinating conjunction.)

_____

2. Elmo and Catalina received the prize for the best essay. They felt good about working as writing partners. (Make a compound sentence by using a semicolon and a conjunctive adverb.)

_____

Chapter 12: Writing Complete Sentences

Review (Form A)

Exercise A   Some of the following word groups are complete sentences; others are sentence fragments or run-on sentences. On the line provided, identify each by writing **S** for sentence, **F** for fragment, or **R** for run-on.

_____ 1. We know that new words are constantly coming into our language.

_____ 2. Some of the new words are slang expressions, these words often do not last very long.

_____ 3. Most of us know at least a few "private" slang expressions.

_____ 4. Slang terms that are used by a small group of people, such as the members of a single family or the students in a particular school.

_____ 5. These words are part of our language only in a limited sense, most speakers of the language do not know them.

_____ 6. Other slang terms do become generally popular.

_____ 7. Like a new hit tune, a new slang word may gain acceptance almost overnight.

_____ 8. Being heard everywhere for a few months, then fading into oblivion.

_____ 9. We can all name slang expressions that have gone out of date, for instance, _right on_ and _groovy_ were popular in our parents' generation.

_____10. In our grandparents' generation, _skidoo_, _ixnay_, and _the cat's pajamas_.

_____11. We may know what these terms mean, we do not usually use them in our own speech.

_____12. The popular slang used in our great-great-grandparents' time being completely unfamiliar to us.

_____13. For instance, most of us today would not like to receive an invitation to a _rout_.

_____14. The usual meaning of _rout_ is "disastrous defeat," once it was also a fashionable slang term for a large party.

_____15. Surprisingly enough, some slang terms endure for generation after generation.

_____16. The word _swell_, meaning "fine" or "good," never accepted as a suitable term for serious speaking or writing.

_____17. Despite its long history of use in informal speech.

_____18. _Con_, meaning "to swindle," is another slang usage that goes back for many years.

Chapter 12: Writing Complete Sentences

Review (Form A)

_____ 19. Everyone realizes that a statement like "He conned me out of two bucks"
is slangy no one would use it in a formal situation.

_____ 20. Thus our language does have a small body of fairly permanent slang
expressions.

Exercise B   Change the punctuation and capitalization in order to eliminate the
sentence fragments and run-on sentences from the following passage. Most, but not all, of
the numbered lines will require a change.

> **Example:** Most of the new words that enter our language
> today are not slang expressions. But scientific or
> technical terms.

1. New scientific discoveries call for new words for example, medicines

2. like penicillin and streptomycin were unheard of sixty years ago. Al-

3. though now we hear their names almost daily. The word *allergy* has been

4. in the language for many years, however, remedies for allergies were

5. discovered only recently. These remedies are called *antihistamines*. A

6. new term. That is now familiar to every hay-fever sufferer. Words for old-

7. fashioned medical techniques go out of use, however. At the same time

8. that words for new techniques come into use. How many people today

9. know what *cupping* means, how many doctors today would write a prescrip-

10. tion mentioning *laudanum*? The name of a once-popular painkiller.

Chapter 12: Writing Complete Sentences

Review (Form B)

Exercise A   Some of the following word groups are complete sentences; others are sentence fragments or run-on sentences. On the line provided, identify each by writing **S** for sentence, **F** for fragment, or **R** for run-on.

_____ 1. Many high school students are beginning to think about their future careers.

_____ 2. With the aid of guidance counselors, beginning to research job opportunities and set career goals.

_____ 3. Some high schools offer vocational training programs to prepare students for the working world, for example, word-processing programs train students to work in the automated office.

_____ 4. Typing is the most essential of all office skills.

_____ 5. A typing or word-processing course is also helpful to college-bound students.

_____ 6. Since most college professors do not accept handwritten papers.

_____ 7. In large cities specialized high schools that are devoted to specific kinds of vocational training.

_____ 8. Performing arts high schools for future entertainers.

_____ 9. Science high schools emphasize training in the sciences while covering traditional academic course work; high schools of music and art require students to take additional courses in music or art.

_____ 10. To attend one of these schools, students must pass a special entrance examination.

_____ 11. My high school has instituted a yearly poll of students' career choices.

_____ 12. Students are asked to complete a questionnaire about their career goals, courses are then designed to meet students' needs.

_____ 13. Some courses including internship programs to give students hands-on experience.

_____ 14. Experience that is very helpful in making a career decision.

_____ 15. My school also offers a series of career nights, each career night provides students with the opportunity to investigate a specific field.

_____ 16. To meet with professionals who know about job possibilities.

_____ 17. In a wide range of fields, such as professional writing, travel and tourism, or real estate.

_____ 18. I generally have a hard time deciding which seminar to attend, I am interested in a number of different kinds of jobs.

Chapter 12: Writing Complete Sentences

Review (Form B)

_____19. I often think that I would like to work in a number of different areas, perhaps a job with diversified responsibilities would suit me.

_____20. Perhaps I'll be like Walter Mitty, a James Thurber character who, in his dreams, makes a career of changing jobs.

Exercise B   The following groups of words are sentence fragments. Each fragment can be made into a complete sentence by removing one word. Find the word that should be removed and cross it out, leaving a complete sentence. You may sometimes need to cross out a comma, as well.

> **Example:** Figure skating, ~~which~~ is a very demanding sport.

1. My friend Felicia, who is a dedicated figure skater.

2. Because of her busy schedule, so she hardly ever has time to spend with me, her best friend.

3. Her skates and leg warmers that are in use every single day, including Saturdays and Sundays.

4. When she must get up at four in the morning and go to practice in that cold, deserted rink, whether she feels like going or not.

5. Since many other sports do not require nearly as many skills as skating.

6. Artistry, stamina, and technical skill, which are all essential to winning the competitions.

7. Two hours of each day that are spent in each of the following activities: ballet lessons, gymnastics lessons, skating lessons, solitary skating practice, public school, private tutoring, and homework.

8. Her constant companion and supporter in her efforts, her mother, who cheerfully drives her from one appointment to another.

9. Because her parents have invested a great deal of money and time in her skating career.

10. Her biggest fan, her father, who not only pays for all the lessons, but also insists on coming to every one of her competitions.

Answer Key

Practice and Reinforcement (1)
Types of Sentence Fragments A

Exercise A

1. V	6. V
2. S	7. S
3. C	8. V
4. C	9. V
5. S	10. C

Exercise B

(Answers will vary. Sample responses are given.)

1. The South had a deep faith in states' rights.
2. South Carolina seceded from the Union.
3. Many slave owners protested the election of Abraham Lincoln.
4. Jefferson Davis, a mild-mannered man, became president of the Confederacy.
5. The issue of slavery was only one of the issues that led to the Civil War.

Practice and Reinforcement (2)
Types of Sentence Fragments B

Exercise A

1. PP	3. VP
2. SC	4. AP

Exercise B

(Answers will vary. Sample responses are given.)

1. When I go to an Indian restaurant, I enjoy tasting the different breads.
2. Fernando bought his lunch at the West Indian takeout.

Practice and Reinforcement (3)
Identifying Run-on Sentences

Exercise A

1. FS	4. CS
2. CS	5. FS
3. FS	

Exercise B

(Answers will vary. Possible responses are given.)

1. I will hear the news on Saturday, but Elmo will find out on Sunday.
2. Elmo and Catalina received the prize for the best essay; therefore, they felt good about working as writing partners.

Chapter Review (Form A)

Exercise A

1. S	11. R
2. R	12. F
3. S	13. S
4. F	14. R
5. R	15. S
6. S	16. F
7. S	17. F
8. F	18. S
9. R	19. R
10. F	20. S

Exercise B

1. New scientific discoveries call for new words. for example, medicines
2. like penicillin and streptomycin were unheard of sixty years ago. Al-
3. though now we hear their names almost daily. The word *allergy* has been
4. in the language for many years. however, remedies for allergies were
5. discovered only recently. These remedies are called *antihistamines*, A
6. new term. That is now familiar to every hay-fever sufferer. Words for old-
7. fashioned medical techniques go out of use, however. At the same time
8. that words for new techniques come into use. How many people today
9. know what *cupping* means. how many doctors today would write a prescrip-
10. tion mentioning *laudanum?* The name of a once-popular painkiller?

Answer Key

Chapter Review (Form B)

Exercise A

1. S
2. F
3. R
4. S
5. S
6. F
7. F
8. F
9. S
10. S
11. S
12. R
13. F
14. F
15. R
16. F
17. F
18. R
19. R
20. S

Exercise B

1. ~~, who~~
2. ~~so~~
3. ~~that~~
4. ~~When~~
5. ~~Since~~
6. ~~, which~~
7. ~~that~~
8. ~~, who~~ (comma optional)
9. ~~Because~~
10. ~~, who~~ (comma optional)

Chapter 13: Writing Effective Sentences

Inserting Words and Phrases

You can combine sentences by taking a key word from one sentence and inserting it into another sentence. When you do this, you may need to delete one or more words. You may also need to change the form of the word you insert.

Original: Hiram Revels was elected to Congress. This was fortunate.

Combined: Fortunately, Hiram Revels was elected to Congress.

You also can combine sentences by reducing one sentence to a prepositional phrase, participial phrase, or appositive phrase and inserting it into the other sentence.

Original: Blanche K. Bruce served in the U.S. Senate from 1875 to 1881. He was an African American Mississippian.

Combined: Blanche K. Bruce, an African American Mississippian, served in the U.S. Senate from 1875 to 1881. [appositive phrase]

Exercise Combine each pair of sentences below by inserting a word, a form of a word, or a group of words from one sentence into the other.

1. Maria Mitchell grew up in a house in Nantucket. She was the daughter of an American astronomer.

   _____

2. Maria grew up in a house on Vestal Street. The house was in Nantucket.

   _____

3. She became famous. Her fame was international.

   _____

4. She was an astronomer. She became well-known.

   _____

5. She discovered a comet. She discovered it by looking through a telescope.

   _____

Chapter 13: Writing Effective Sentences

Using Compound Subjects and Verbs

You can combine sentences by using compound subjects and verbs. Just look for sentences that have the same subject or the same verb. Then use coordinating conjunctions (such as *and, but, or, nor, for,* or *yet*) to make a compound subject, a compound verb, or both.

Original: Early African American aviators faced obstacles.
Early African American aviators accomplished great feats in the air.

Complete sentence: Early African American aviators faced obstacles yet accomplished great feats in the air.

Exercise   Combine each of the following pairs of sentences by using coordinating conjunctions to combine subjects and verbs.

1. The interest of African Americans in early flight has been ignored. The contributions of African Americans to early flight have been ignored.

_____

2. Bessie Coleman was an African American pioneer in flight. James Herman Banning was an African American pioneer in flight.

_____

3. Corporate support was not available to early African American pilots. Good airplanes were not available to early African American pilots.

_____

4. Nevertheless, African American pilots broke records. African American pilots performed stunts. African American pilots helped advance American aviation.

_____

5. James Herman Banning completed a transcontinental flight in 1932. Thomas C. Allen completed a transcontinental flight in 1932.

_____

Chapter 13: Writing Effective Sentences

Creating a Compound Sentence

If the thoughts in two sentences are related to one another and are equal in importance, you can combine the sentences to form a **compound sentence**. A compound sentence is two or more simple sentences joined by a comma and a coordinating conjunction, a semicolon, or a semicolon and a conjunctive adverb.

Original: Mickey Rooney was a child star. He was once the most popular film star in America.

Revised: Mickey Rooney was a child star, **and** he was once the most popular film star in America. [comma and coordinating conjunction]

Mickey Rooney was a child star; he was once the most popular film star in America. [semicolon]

Mickey Rooney was a child star; **moreover,** he was once the most popular film star in America. [semicolon and conjunctive adverb]

Exercise   Combine each of the following pairs of sentences to create compound sentences.

1. Rooney suffered many career setbacks. In his sixties he became popular as a character actor.

   _____

2. Bette Davis was nominated for many Academy Awards. She was the first woman to win two.

   _____

3. Davis never considered herself beautiful. She proved herself one of the best dramatic stars of Hollywood.

   _____

4. The studio that signed Davis for her first film in 1931 dropped her. It was thought that she lacked appeal.

   _____

5. Humphrey Bogart did not have the traits of the standard male star of his day. He became symbolic of a type of anti-hero.

   _____

Chapter 13: Writing Effective Sentences

Creating a Complex Sentence

If two sentences are unequal in importance, you can combine them by forming a complex sentence. A **complex sentence** includes one independent clause and one or more subordinate clauses.

You can make a sentence into an **adjective clause** by replacing its subject with *who, which,* or *that*. Then you can use the adjective clause to give information about a noun or a pronoun in another sentence.

> **Original:** Comets are heavenly bodies. Comets are made up of gases.
>
> **Revised:** Comets are heavenly bodies that are made up of gases.

You can turn one sentence into an **adverb clause** and combine it with another sentence. The adverb clause may modify a verb, an adjective, or another adverb in the sentence that it is attached to.

> **Original:** The gases were frozen. They formed giant snowballs.
>
> **Revised:** When the gases were frozen, they formed giant snowballs.

You can make a sentence into a **noun clause** by adding a word such as *that, how, what, whatever, who,* or *whoever*. Then you can insert it into a sentence just like an ordinary noun. When you combine the sentences, you may need to delete or change some words.

> **Original:** Giovanni Schiaparelli noticed the Swift-Tuttle Comet. He noticed the comet crossing the earth's orbit around the sun.
>
> **Revised:** Giovanni Schiaparelli noticed that the Swift-Tuttle Comet crosses the earth's orbit around the sun.

Exercise   Combine each of the following pairs of sentences by creating adjective clauses, adverb clauses, or noun clauses from one sentence and inserting them into the other sentence.

1. Native Americans of the Plains spent most of the year divided into hunting bands. The bands roamed constantly in search of buffalo.

   _____

2. The cold weather and the end of the harvest arrived. The bands followed the buffalo.

   _____

3. The Devil's Medicine Man was the name of one hunting band. It probably consisted of only twenty or thirty tepees.

   _____

4. Bands met up during their search. They camped together.

   _____

Chapter 13: Writing Effective Sentences

Using Parallel Structure

When you join several equal or related ideas in a sentence, it's important to balance the structure of your sentence parts. For example, you balance an adjective with an adjective, a phrase with a phrase, and a clause with a clause. This kind of balance is called **parallel structure.**

Not parallel: Quickly but with thoroughness, the senator answered the question.

Parallel: Quickly but thoroughly, the senator answered the question. [two parallel adverbs: *quickly, thoroughly*]

Exercise   Revise each of the following sentences by putting the ideas in parallel form.

1. Evaluate the television programs you watch by considering their purpose, presentation, and having an educational value.

   _____

2. Singing in an opera requires more training than in a school choir.

   _____

3. A hike in the Grand Canyon would enable you to see more than just driving through it.

   _____

4. To travel by camper and renting a beach house are popular American vacations.

   _____

5. Flying an airplane requires more skill than a car.

   _____

6. The heroine of *O Pioneers!* convinces her brothers to mortgage the farm and make an investment in more land.

   _____

7. Energetically yet with grace, Maurice Hines tap-danced.

   _____

8. Two goals of the NAACP were to build up membership and encouraging nonviolent reform.

   _____

9. If you own a car, knowing how to fix a flat tire is as important as whether you know how to fill the gas tank.

   _____

10. He thought living in Shanghai was better than Beijing.

   _____

Chapter 13: Writing Effective Sentences

Stringy and Wordy Sentences

A **stringy sentence** has too many independent clauses strung together with coordinating conjunctions such as *and* or *but*. To fix a stringy sentence, you can break the sentence into two or more shorter sentences or turn some of the independent clauses into subordinate clauses or phrases.

> **Stringy:** People come to the United States from Korea, and they come from India, and they come from the Philippines.
>
> **Revised:** People come to the United States from Korea, India, and the Philippines.

To make your sentences less wordy, don't use more words than you need to; don't use fancy words where simple ones will do; and don't repeat words or ideas unless it's absolutely necessary.

Exercise A   Revise each of the following sentences by breaking them into two or more sentences or by turning independent clauses into subordinate clauses and phrases.

1. The first immigrants came mostly from England, but some came from Ireland, and some came from France.

   _____

2. The first Jewish Americans arrived in the 1600s, but many did not come until the mid-1800s, and by 1920 four million Jewish immigrants had reached America.

   _____

3. Large numbers of Chinese arrived at the time of the California gold rush in 1849, and they hoped to find gold.

   _____

4. Many Irish arrived after the potato famine in Ireland, and some of them became farmers, and some of them worked in factories.

   _____

Exercise B   Revise the following wordy sentences by eliminating any words that are not necessary or by using simple words instead of fancy ones.

1. One large group of immigrants did not want to come to this country and were brought involuntarily.

   _____

2. Slave traders went to West Africa and captured people on the western part of the continent.

   _____

Chapter 13: Writing Effective Sentences

Varying Your Sentences

Many sentences begin with a subject followed by a verb. You can use the following methods to vary this type of beginning.

Use a single-word modifier: **Carefully,** Hasan revised his paper.

    Use a phrase: **With care,** Hasan revised his paper. [prepositional phrase]

                      Writing quickly, Hasan revised his paper. [participial phrase]

Use a subordinate clause: **Because he had a new idea,** Hasan revised his paper. [adverb clause]

Another way to vary sentences is by using a variety of simple, compound, complex, and compound-complex sentences in your paragraphs.

Exercise A   On the lines provided, revise each of the following sentences. Follow the directions in parentheses to vary each sentence beginning.

1. Luis studied the history of basketball in social studies class. (Use a phrase.)

_____

2. A game similar to basketball was invented in Mexico before basketball was ever played in the United States. (Use a subordinate clause.)

_____

3. A form of basketball was invented by the Olmec people of ancient Mexico, which is interesting. (Use a single-word modifier.)

_____

4. They played an early form of the game called *pok-ta-pok* by shooting a rubber ball through a ring. (Use a phrase.)

_____

Exercise B   On the lines provided, revise the following paragraph to create variety in sentence structure. You may add, delete, or change words as necessary.

      Sports have come from countries around the world. Bowling was probably

first played in Egypt. Wrestling probably began in Egypt or Mesopotamia.

Boxing had its beginning in early Greece. Bullfighting originated in Crete. Tennis

began in France.

_____

_____

_____

_____

Review (Form A)

Exercise A   Each of the following five sentences begins with the subject. Underline the word or group of words that could be placed at the beginning of the sentence to create sentence variety.

> **Example:** The fate of a television show is often determined <u>by viewer ratings</u>.

1. A show is almost certain to be dropped if its rating is very low.

2. A viewer rating is not a measure of the show's quality, of course.

3. The rating, as we all know, merely indicates how many people are tuned in to the show.

4. The rating unfortunately does not indicate how much these people like the show.

5. A rating usually does not even tell whether the people are paying attention to the show.

Exercise B   Using sentence combining techniques, rewrite the following sentence pairs. Follow the directions given in parentheses.

> **Example:** I planned to stay home last weekend. I was going to study for a history test. (Reduce the second sentence to a phrase beginning with *to study*, and combine into one sentence.)
>
> I planned to stay home last weekend <u>to study for a history test.</u>

1. I planned to study. I turned down an invitation to go skating. (Combine into a simple sentence that begins with *Planning*.) _____

   _____

2. Iris Barino called me up Saturday evening. Iris is my best friend. (Rewrite as a simple sentence, reducing the second sentence to an appositive phrase.) _____

   _____

   _____

3. She asked me to go to an Audrey Hepburn movie. The movie was playing at the Rialto. (Combine into a complex sentence, using the word *that*.) _____

   _____

   _____

4. I stuck to my resolution. I stayed home. (Combine into a simple sentence with a compound verb.) _____

   _____

Chapter 13: Writing Effective Sentences

Review (Form A)

5. I arrived at school Monday morning. I was well prepared and full of confidence.

   (Combine into a complex sentence, beginning with *When*.) _____

   _____

Exercise C   The sentences in the passage below are unnecessarily short and choppy. On the lines provided, use subordinate clauses, compound verbs, and any other means you wish, to combine the ideas in the passage into smoother sentences.

      Kite-flying is a popular sport. It is popular with young and old alike. Kites do not often serve useful purposes. They are pretty to watch. They are fun to fly. Kites have changed little in design over the years. Some new kites are made of plastic instead of paper. A typical kite is diamond-shaped. It has cross-bars of wood for support. The wood is lightweight balsa wood. This kind of kite requires a tail in order to fly. The tail is usually made of strips of rag. They are knotted together.

_____

_____

_____

_____

_____

_____

_____

_____

_____

_____

_____

_____

Chapter 13: Writing Effective Sentences

Review (Form B)

Exercise A   Each of the following five sentences begins with the subject. Underline the word or group of words that could be placed at the beginning of the sentence to create sentence variety.

> **Example:** The campers gathered on the playing field <u>after the whistle had sounded.</u>

1. The referee calmly read the rules of the game.

2. The team members, eager to start playing, agreed to abide by the referee's decisions.

3. The team members huddled to discuss strategy with their captains.

4. Rain unfortunately put a damper on the afternoon's activity.

5. The campers ran back to their bunks as it began to pour.

Exercise B   Using sentence combining techniques, rewrite the following sentence pairs. Follow the directions given in parentheses.

> **Example:** Camouflage is a form of self-defense. Camouflage protects many animal species. (Combine into a complex sentence using the word *that*.)
> <u>Camouflage is a form of self-defense that protects</u>
> <u>many animal species.</u>

1. The hermit crab picks sea anemones from rocks. It plants them on its shell for camouflage. (Combine into a simple sentence with a compound verb.) _____

   _____

2. The chameleon blends into its surroundings. It changes its color. (Reduce the second sentence to a phrase and combine into one sentence.) _____

   _____

3. Winter approaches. The brown coat of a weasel turns snowy white. (Combine into a complex sentence, beginning with *As*.) _____

   _____

4. Shrimps live in seaweed, and they can match the color of the seaweed. (Rewrite as a complex sentence, using the words *in which*.) _____

   _____

Review (Form B)

5. Mimicry may help an animal survive. Mimicry is a form of protective

coloration. (Combine into a complex sentence, using the word *which*.) _____

_____

_____

Exercise C   The sentences in the passage below are unnecessarily short and choppy. On the lines provided, use subordinate clauses, compound verbs, and any other means you wish, to combine the ideas in the passage into smooth sentences.

Poor Richard's Almanack was written and published by Benjamin Franklin. He

wrote it under the name Richard Saunders. Richard Saunders was supposedly an

impoverished astronomer. "Poor Richard" was like other publishers of almanacs

in colonial America. He noted the holidays. He forecast the weather. He offered

practical advice. He printed poems. He printed jokes. He printed odd facts. Most

importantly, he printed clever proverbs or sayings. These sayings expressed his

own philosophy of life. Poor Richard was misnamed. The almanac prospered. So

did Benjamin Franklin. He was a wealthy man by the age of forty-two. He could

afford to retire.

_____

_____

_____

_____

_____

_____

_____

_____

_____

_____

_____

Answer Key

Practice and Reinforcement (1)
Inserting Words and Phrases

Exercise

(Answers will vary. Possible responses are given.)

1. Maria Mitchell, the daughter of an American astronomer, grew up in a house in Nantucket.
2. Maria grew up in a house on Vestal Street in Nantucket.
3. She became internationally famous.
4. She became a well-known astronomer.
5. She discovered a comet by looking through a telescope.

Practice and Reinforcement (2)
Using Compound Subjects and Verbs

Exercise

(Answers will vary. Possible responses are given.)

1. The interest in and contributions of African Americans to early flight have been ignored.
2. Bessie Coleman and James Herman Banning were African American pioneers in flight.
3. Corporate support and good airplanes were not available to early African American pilots.
4. Nevertheless, African American pilots broke records, performed stunts, and helped advance American aviation.
5. James Herman Banning and Thomas C. Allen completed a transcontinental flight in 1932.

Practice and Reinforcement (3)
Creating a Compound Sentence

(Answers will vary. Possible responses are given.)

1. Rooney suffered many career setbacks, but in his sixties, he became popular as a character actor.
2. Bette Davis was nominated for many Oscars; she was the first woman to win two.
3. Davis never considered herself beautiful; nevertheless, she proved herself one of the best dramatic stars of Hollywood.
4. The studio that signed Davis for her first film in 1931 dropped her; it was thought that she lacked appeal.

5. Humphrey Bogart did not have the traits of the standard male star of his day; consequently, he became symbolic of a type of anti-hero.

Practice and Reinforcement (4)
Creating a Complex Sentence

Exercise

(Answers will vary. Possible responses are given.)

1. Native Americans of the Plains spent most of the year divided into hunting hands that roamed constantly in search of buffalo.
2. As soon as the cold weather and the end of the harvest arrived, the bands followed the buffalo.
3. The Devil's Medicine Man, which was the name of one hunting band, probably consisted of only twenty or thirty tepees.
4. When bands met up during their search, they camped together.

Practice and Reinforcement (5)
Using Parallel Structure

Exercise

(Answers will vary. Possible responses are given.)

1. Evaluate the television programs you watch by considering their purpose, presentation, and educational value.
2. Singing in an opera requires more training than singing in a school choir.
3. Hiking in the Grand Canyon would enable you to see more than just driving through it.
4. Traveling by camper and renting a beach house are popular American vacations.
5. Flying an airplane requires more skill than driving a car.
6. The heroine of *O Pioneers!* convinces her brothers to mortgage the farm and invest in more land.
7. Energetically yet gracefully, Maurice Hines tap-danced.
8. Two goals of the NAACP were building up membership and encouraging nonviolent reform.

Answer Key

9. If you own a car, knowing how to fix a flat tire is as important as knowing how to fill the gas tank.

10. He thought living in Shanghai was better than living in Beijing.

Practice and Reinforcement (6)
Stringy and Wordy Sentences

Exercise A

(Answers will vary. Possible responses are given.)

1. The first immigrants came mostly from England. Some came from Ireland and France.

2. The first Jewish Americans arrived in the 1600s, but many did not come until the mid-1800s. By 1920 four million Jewish immigrants had reached America.

3. Large numbers of Chinese who hoped to find gold arrived in 1849 when the California gold rush occurred.

4. When the many Irish arrived after the potato famine in Ireland, some of them became farmers, and some of them worked in factories.

Exercise B

(Answers will vary. Possible responses are given.)

1. One large group of immigrants did not come voluntarily.

2. Slave traders captured people in West Africa.

Practice and Reinforcement (7)
Varying Your Sentences

Exercise A

(Answers will vary. Possible responses are given.)

1. In social studies class, Luis studied the history of basketball.

2. Before basketball was ever played in the United States, a game similar to basketball was invented in Mexico.

3. Interestingly, a form of basketball was invented by the Olmec people of ancient Mexico.

4. Shooting a rubber ball through a ring, they played an early form of the game called *pok-ta-pok.*

Exercise B

(Answers will vary. A possible response is given.)

Sports that we play today were invented in countries all around the world. Bowling was probably first played in Egypt, while wrestling probably began in Egypt or Mesopotamia. Boxing had its beginning in early Greece, while bullfighting originated in Crete. The sport of tennis began in France.

Chapter Review (Form A)

Exercise A

1. A show is almost certain to be dropped <u>if its rating is very low</u>.

2. A viewer rating is not a measure of the show's quality, <u>of course</u>.

3. The rating, <u>as we all know</u>, merely indicates how many people are tuned in to the show.

4. The rating <u>unfortunately</u> does not indicate how much these people like the show.

5. A rating <u>usually</u> does not even tell whether the people are paying attention to the show.

Exercise B

1. Planning to study, I turned down an invitation to go skating.

2. Iris Barino, my best friend, called me up Saturday evening.

3. She asked me to go to an Audrey Hepburn movie that was playing at the Rialto.

4. I stuck to my resolution and stayed home.

5. When I arrived at school Monday morning, I was well prepared and full of confidence.

Exercise C

(Answers will vary. A possible response is given.)

Kite-flying is a sport that is popular with young and old alike. Kites do not often serve useful purposes, but they are pretty to watch and fun to fly. While some new kites are made of plastic instead of paper, kites have changed little in design over the years. A typical kite is diamond-shaped and has crossbars of lightweight balsa wood for support. In order to fly, this kind of kite requires a tail, usually made of strips of rag that have been knotted together.

Answer Key

Chapter Review (Form B)

Exercise A

1. The referee <u>calmly</u> read the rules of the game.
2. The team members, <u>eager to start playing</u>, agreed to abide by the referee's decisions.
3. The team members huddled <u>to discuss strategy with their captains</u>.
4. Rain <u>unfortunately</u> put a damper on the afternoon's activity.
5. The campers ran back to their bunks <u>as it began to pour</u>.

Exercise B

1. The hermit crab picks sea anemones from rocks and plants them on its shell for camouflage.
2. The chameleon blends into its surroundings by changing its color.
3. As winter approaches, the brown coat of a weasel turns snowy white.
4. Shrimps can match the color of the seaweed in which they live.
5. Mimicry, which is a form of protective coloration, may help an animal survive.

Exercise C

(Answers will vary. A possible response is given.)

Poor Richard's Almanack was written and published by Benjamin Franklin under the name Richard Saunders, supposedly an impoverished astronomer. Like other publishers of almanacs in colonial America, "Poor Richard" noted the holidays, forecast the weather, and offered practical advice. He printed poems, jokes, and odd facts. Most importantly, he printed clever proverbs, or sayings that expressed his own philosophy of life. Poor Richard was misnamed, for the almanac prospered. By the age of forty-two, Benjamin Franklin was a wealthy man who could afford to retire.

Name _____ Date _____ Class _____

The Tree of Language

Before about 3000 B.C. an unknown people in central or southern Asia spoke a language now known as **Proto-Indo-European.** That language is the distant ancestor of English and of many other languages. The languages derived from Proto-Indo-European are known as the Indo-European languages. The following chart shows part of the Indo-European family tree.

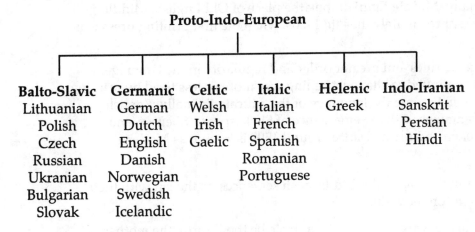

Proto-Indo-European

Balto-Slavic	Germanic	Celtic	Italic	Helenic	Indo-Iranian
Lithuanian	German	Welsh	Italian	Greek	Sanskrit
Polish	Dutch	Irish	French		Persian
Czech	English	Gaelic	Spanish		Hindi
Russian	Danish		Romanian		
Ukranian	Norwegian		Portuguese		
Bulgarian	Swedish				
Slovak	Icelandic				

We know that these languages are related because they share common forms. Notice, for example, how similar the words for *three* are in these Indo-European languages:

Dutch	drie	German	drei	Gothic	thri
Lithuanian	tri	Celtic	tri	Latin	tres
Greek	trias	Persian	thri	Sanskrit	tryas

Exercise   Each group of words below includes one from a non-Indo-European language. Study each group of words. Find the word that is *least* like the other words in the group. Cross out that word to show that its language is not part of the Indo-European family.

1. English—me   Dutch—mij   Chinese—wo
   Latin—me   Persian—me   Lithuanian—manen

2. English—seven   Swahili—saba   Gothic—sibun
   Latin—septem   Sanskrit—sapta   Dutch—zeven

3. English—brother   German—bruder   Lithuanian—brolis
   Greek—phrater   Arabic—ekh   Celtic—brathair

4. English—night   French—nuit   Italian—notte
   Spanish—noche   Greek—nuktós   Korean—pam

5. English—mother   Persian—matar   Greek—meter
   Sanskrit—matar   Chinese—muchin   Dutch—moeder

Chapter 14: English: Origins and Uses

The History of English

The history of the English language is divided into three periods.

Old English was the dominant language in England until around 1066, when the Normans, a French-speaking people, conquered England.

When French became the language of the government, this influenced and changed the English language. Gradually, **Middle English** took the place of Old English. Middle English was spoken until approximately the late 1400s, when the first printing press was set up in England.

With the printing press came rules and greater order and regularity in the language. Although pronunciation continued to change, spelling was more or less fixed by printing. Also, English had once again become the language of the educated. Finally, English became a major literary language with the emergence of Shakespeare, Spenser, and Milton. The language spoken and printed since around 1500 is known as **Modern English.**

Exercise A   Draw arrows to match the Old English sentences on the left with their Modern English translations on the right.

1. Bethlem hattæ seo burh ðe Crist on geboren wes.

2. Hwæt sceal ic singan?

3. Hal wes þu, folde, fira modor.

4. Wæs se grimma gæst Grendel haten.

5. Leoht eastan com, beorht beacen Godes.

a. Hale be thou, earth, the mother of men.

b. Bethlehem was the town (burg) that Christ was born in.

c. Light came from the east, God's bright beacon.

d. What shall I sing?

e. The grim guest was named Grendel.

Exercise B   Some Middle English is so close to Modern English that it can be read fairly easily by a Modern English speaker. Try your own hand at "translating" some lines from Middle English. Work with a classmate or in a small group. Translate into Modern English the following lines from Geoffrey Chaucer's poem *The Knight's Tale*. Write your own line-by-line Modern English translations on the lines provided. (Hints: The word *whilom* means "formerly" or "in the old days." A *duc* is a "duke." *Atthenes* is the city of "Athens." The word *highte* means "called.")

1. Whilom, as olde stories tellen us, _____

2. Ther was a duc that highte Theseus; _____

3. Of Atthenes he was lord and governour, _____

4. And in his tyme swich a conquerour, _____

5. That grette was ther noon under the sonne. _____

Chapter 14: English: Origins and Uses

Modern English

Throughout its history, English has borrowed words from other languages. During the early Middle English period, French was the language used in government, in the schools, and among merchants. At this time so many French words entered the language that it is sometimes easier to think about what English words were *not* adopted from French. These native English words have to do with simple, everyday matters. For example, of all the numerals, only *second* is borrowed. Of all the outer parts of the body, only *face* and *palm* are borrowed.

In the 1500s and 1600s, during the English Renaissance, many Greek and Latin words entered English. Words borrowed from Latin were often legal and political terms such as *alibi*, *propaganda*, and *ultimatum* and scientific and medical terms such as *fulcrum*, *nucleus*, *pendulum*, and *serum*.

During the 1700s and 1800s, England became a world power. English people boasted that the sun never set on their empire. At that time, words entered English from Asia, from Africa, from the Americas, and from other parts of Europe.

Two other major influences on American English have been the languages of Native Americans and the various African dialects spoken by those who were brought here as slaves.

Exercise A   The following word pairs are closely related. One word in each pair is of English origin. The other was borrowed from French after the Norman Conquest. Look up each word in a dictionary to determine its language of origin. Write **F** next to the word that is of French origin and **E** next to the word that is of English origin.

1. cycle _____ wheel _____   6. stool _____ chair _____

2. finish _____ end _____   7. labor _____ work _____

3. edifice _____ building _____   8. vision _____ dream _____

4. appear _____ seem _____   9. multitude _____ crowd _____

5. stead _____ place _____   10. king _____ royal _____

Exercise B   Draw arrows to match the words on the left with their origins on the right.

1. robot   a. from the Czech word *robota*, "work"

2. dungaree   b. from the Tongan (Polynesian) word *tabu*

3. tycoon   c. from the Latin word for "taste"

4. taboo   d. from the Hindi word *dungri*

5. gusto   e. from the Japanese word *taikun*, the title of
                         a Shogun, or powerful general

Name _____ Date _____ Class _____

Formal and Informal English

Whenever you write or speak, you should use language that is right for the occasion.
Formal English is like formal dress—you use it when the occasion is important enough to
demand that you think twice about what you say or how you appear. For example, you
would use formal English for a speech at graduation, in a wedding invitation, or for a
report. **Informal English**, like informal dress, is appropriate for less serious occasions, like
everyday conversation and personal letters.

Exercise   The following paragraphs are from a report on holiday cooking around the
world. Rewrite the paragraph on the lines below to make the language more appropriate.

Here are some of the most awesome holiday eats from all over the world.

First, for the main dishes, there's piroshki. These zazzy little meat pastries are

eaten on any holiday in Russia. There is paella, which is eaten in Spain on any

festive occasion. When you get down to the nitty-gritty, all there is to paella is

some seafood and rice, but people go wild for it. Last but not least, there's kalbi

j'im, a traditional dish of simmered beef short ribs eaten on New Year's Day in

Korea.

What are the toppers? Holiday desserts from around the world include

buñuelos, Mexican fried pastries eaten on Christmas—a real favorite with kids.

Another special holiday dessert is ugat matzot, a layer cake wolfed down on

Passover in Israel. Kestenki, chestnut cookies from Bulgaria, are a real **knock-out**

at the end of any feed.

_____

_____

_____

_____

_____

_____

_____

_____

_____

_____

_____

Chapter 14: English: Origins and Uses

Choosing the Right Synonym

Using **synonyms**, different words that have similar meanings, is a way to bring variety to your writing. But be sure to choose synonyms that say exactly what you want to say. Every word has its own shade of meaning, and some words are more precise than others.

To avert suspicion, the thief told an *intended* lie.

To avert suspicion, the thief told a *deliberate* lie.

The words *deliberate* and *intended* are synonyms, but *deliberate* is more appropriate and precise in this context.

Exercise   Each of the following sentences contains an italicized word that does not quite fit the meaning of the sentence. Rewrite each sentence, replacing the italicized word with the synonym in parentheses that best fits the context.

1. Cletha hesitated to bring up such a *subtle* matter in front of her grandmother. (delicate, diplomatic)

   _____

2. The elderly woman thanked Paulo for his *favor*. (grace, kindness)

   _____

3. When Giorgio felt his toes, he realized they were completely *dull*. (dead, numb)

   _____

4. Tanya thought she was funny, but she was actually *corrosive*. (sarcastic, ironic)

   _____

5. Calling quickly for professional help is almost always a *balanced* thing to do in an emergency. (levelheaded, discreet)

   _____

6. Olivia was just barely able to *watch* two shapes in the darkness. (identify, examine)

   _____

7. Pluto is at the *utmost* reaches of our solar system. (outermost, uttermost)

   _____

8. Early in the trip, they decided to *convert* their destination. (shift, change)

   _____

9. They crossed a wide *extent* of desert. (expanse, distance)

   _____

10. After knocking on the wrong door, Buford turned red with *distress*. (discomposure, embarrassment)

   _____

Denotation and Connotation

The **denotation** of a word is its dictionary meaning. The **connotations** are the associations, attitudes, or feelings that are suggested by a word. For example, the terms *expensive* and *high-priced* have the same denotation. However, they differ in their connotations. *High-priced* suggests something that costs more than it is worth. *Expensive* suggests something that costs a lot, but not necessarily more than it is worth. To communicate effectively, choose words that have appropriate connotations.

Exercise A   In each sentence below, the words in parentheses have the same denotation but different connotations. Underline the item in parentheses that best fits the meaning of the sentence.

> **Example:** The king (stated, proclaimed) that there would be a royal feast. [*Proclaimed* suggests a great event or message; *stated* could apply to lesser or more everyday messages.]

1. The army band (walked, marched) across the drill field.

2. When Marta heard the tragic news, she (cried, wailed) with grief.

3. The polite children (munched, wolfed down) their sandwiches.

4. In a matter-of-fact voice, Maika (said, exclaimed) that the train was running late.

5. Elena prefers (half-cooked, rare) steaks.

Exercise B   Decide whether each word or phrase below has positive, neutral, or negative connotations. On the line provided, write **P** for positive, **NU** for neutral, or **NG** for negative.

1. _____ looked into   _____ snooped

2. _____ asked   _____ whined

3. _____ fashionable   _____ trendy

4. _____ decrepit   _____ old

5. _____ tasteless   _____ bland

6. _____ colorful   _____ gaudy

7. _____ naive   _____ innocent

8. _____ laughed   _____ snorted

9. _____ smart   _____ brilliant

10. _____ tired   _____ exhausted

Chapter 14: English: Origins and Uses

Jargon and Gobbledygook

Jargon is language that has a special meaning for a particular group of people, such as people who share the same profession, occupation, hobby, or field of study. For example, you might use the word *strike* to mean "to hit." Yet, a bowler would use *strike* to mean "to knock down all ten pins," and a geologist might use the word *strike* to refer to the direction of a horizontal line in a bed of rock.

Gobbledygook is a type of jargon that consists of wordy, puffed-up language. Users of gobbledygook choose big words over short ones, difficult words over simple ones. They also use vague, pretentious language. Often the users of gobbledygook get tripped up in their own pretentiousness because their language becomes ridiculously awkward.

> **Gobbledygook:** Excessive hurrying yields deleterious effects.
>
> **Simple English:** Haste makes waste.

Exercise A   Use a dictionary to find out what the word *string* means in the jargon of each of the following fields. Write the meaning on the line provided.

1. Computer science _____

2. Architecture _____

3. Music _____

4. Football _____

Exercise B   Rewrite each of the following examples of gobbledygook in clear, precise language. Use a dictionary to help with word meanings.

1. The smallest unit of monetary worth that is saved is the smallest unit of monetary worth that is earned.

_____

2. Far superior is the act of conferring upon than being conferred upon.

_____

3. The carnivorous feline animal is in receipt of nine existences.

_____

4. That which is simply and effortlessly obtained is also simply and effortlessly misplaced.

_____

5. One fruit of the apple tree ingested on a daily basis has the efficacious effect of allaying frequent visitations by medically skilled practitioners.

_____

Mixed Figures of Speech and Clichés

A **mixed figure of speech** occurs when you begin with one figurative comparison and suddenly switch to another.

> **Mixed:** The book is a treasure chest of wisdom in which you will find a greenhouse of rare flowers to decorate your speech. [Two comparisons are combined: *treasure chest* and *greenhouse*.]
>
> **Better:** The book is a treasure chest of wisdom in which you will find a hoard of verbal gems to adorn your speech.

A **cliché** is an expression so overused that it has become dull and nearly meaningless. Examples of clichés are *as cold as ice* and *as busy as a bee*. Like clichés, **tired words** are words that are overused and almost meaningless, such as *nice, fine, pretty,* and *great*. Examples of tired phrases include *Let me say in closing* and *be that as it may*. When you write, you should strive to use fresh words and comparisons.

Exercise A   Rewrite each sentence to eliminate the mixed figure of speech.

1. Her path was strewn with serious problems that threatened to engulf her completely.

    _____

2. She promised to put her nose to the grindstone to shave the fat from the budget.

    _____

3. Like a bunch of buzzards, the media landed on the victim and refused to stop barking and baying until he talked with them.

    _____

4. His climb up the ladder of success was nipped in the bud.

    _____

Exercise B   Underline the cliché or tired word or phrase in each sentence below. Then, on the lines provided, rewrite the sentence to eliminate it.

1. The victim appeared to be as dead as a doornail.

    _____

2. At this point in time, the police do not wish to make a statement.

    _____

3. This case might provide clues to another murder; if so, police will kill two birds with one stone.

    _____

4. Police will leave no stone unturned until this case is solved.

    _____

Chapter 14: English: Origins and Uses

Review (Form A)

Exercise A   The following are statements about the English language. On the lines provided, write **T** if the statement is true and **F** if the statement is false.

_____ 1. Denotations are associations or attitudes and feelings about a word.

_____ 2. English came from a language family known as Proto-Indo-European.

_____ 3. The Normans invaded England and brought with them their French language.

_____ 4. The invention of the printing press caused speakers to begin using Old English.

_____ 5. English has borrowed words from languages all around the globe.

_____ 6. Jargon is language spoken in one particular region of the United States.

_____ 7. The connotation of a word is its dictionary meaning.

_____ 8. Formal language is language appropriate for everyday conversation and personal letters.

_____ 9. Although not appropriate for every writing situation, writers should strive to use gobbledygook where possible.

_____10. One way we know that several languages came from the same Proto-Indo-European language family is that the languages share cognates, or common forms.

Exercise B   The following loan words have become part of American English. Use a dictionary to define each word and to identify the language from which it is borrowed.

1. charivari _____

2. depot _____

3. bureau _____

4. chintz _____

5. cruller _____

Exercise C   On the line provided, identify each word or phrase. Write **J** for jargon, **MFS** for mixed figure of speech, **T** for tired word, **G** for gobbledygook, and **C** for cliché.

_____ 1. as happy as a clam

_____ 2. wonderful

_____ 3. like a grain of sand crying out in the wilderness

_____ 4. beat, as used in music

_____ 5. a supernatural apparition of ghostly appearance

Chapter 14: English: Origins and Uses

Review (Form B)

Exercise A   Draw arrows to match the following terms with their definitions.

1. jargon   a. language appropriate for everyday conversation

2. Old English   b. the dictionary meaning of a word

3. connotations   c. the language family from which English, French, Russian, Latin, Greek, and many other languages are descended

4. informal English   d. language appropriate for serious, dignified occasions

5. Proto-Indo-European   e. the language spoken in England from around 1066 until the late 1400s

6. gobbledygook   f. the special language of a profession or field of activity

7. clichés   g. wordy, puffed-up language

8. denotation   h. the dominant language in England until around 1066

9. formal English   i. the meanings suggested by or associated with a word

10. Middle English   j. expressions that are overused or tired

Exercise B   Rewrite each of the following examples of gobbledygook in clear, precise language. Use a dictionary to help with word meanings.

1. Precipitousness occasions depletion. _____

   _____

2. The sum total of matter which scintillates is not necessarily bullion. _____

   _____

Exercise C   On the line provided, identify each word or phrase. Write **J** for jargon, **MFS** for mixed figure of speech, **T** for a tired word, **G** for gobbledygook, or **C** for cliché.

_____ 1. good

_____ 2. so utterly immobile as to be stationary

_____ 3. as quiet as a mouse

_____ 4. floating on a ship of fools

_____ 5. cut, as used in baseball

Answer Key

Practice and Reinforcement (1)
The Tree of Language

Exercise A

1. ~~Chinese—wo~~
2. ~~Swahili—saba~~
3. ~~Arabic—ekh~~
4. ~~Korean—pam~~
5. ~~Chinese—muchin~~

Practice and Reinforcement (2)
The History of English

Exercise A

1. Bethlem hattæ seo burh ǎe Crist on geboren wes.
2. Hæwt sceal ic singan?
3. Hal wes þu, folde, fira modor.
4. Wæs se grimma gæst Grendel haten.
5. Leoht eastan com, beorht beacen Godes.

a. Hale be thou, earth, the mother of men.
b. Bethlehem was the town (burg) that Christ was born in.
c. Light came from the east, God's bright beacon.
d. What shall I sing?
e. The grim guest was named Grendel.

Exercise B
(Answers will vary. Possible responses are given.)

1. Formerly, as old stories tell us,
2. There was a duke named Theseus;
3. Of Athens he was lord and governor,
4. And in his time such a conqueror,
5. That there was none greater than he under the sun.

Practice and Reinforcement (3)
Modern English

Exercise A

1. cycle F, wheel E
2. finish F, end E
3. edifice F, building E
4. appear F, seem E
5. stead E, place F
6. stool E, chair F
7. labor F, work E
8. vision F, dream E
9. multitude F, crowd E
10. king E, royal F

Exercise B

1. a
2. d
3. e
4. b
5. c

Practice and Reinforcement (4)
Formal and Informal English

Exercise

(Answers will vary. A possible response is given.)

Holiday dishes are mouth-watering all over the world. One special holiday main dish is piroshki. This dish, which consists of little meat pastries, is eaten on any holiday in Russia. Another delicious main dish is paella, a seafood and rice casserole, eaten on any festive occasion in Spain. A special main dish from the Far East is kalbi j'im, a traditional dish of simmered beef short ribs eaten on New Year's Day in Korea.

Holiday desserts are equally delicious and interesting. These desserts include buñuelos, Mexican fried pastries eaten on Christmas—a favorite with children. Another special holiday dessert is ugat matzot, a layer cake eaten on Passover in Israel. Kestenki, chestnut cookies from Bulgaria, are also a delicious ending to any holiday meal.

Answer Key

Practice and Reinforcement (5)
Choosing the Right Synonym

Exercise

1. Cletha hesitated to bring up such a delicate matter in front of her grandmother.
2. The elderly woman thanked Paulo for his kindness.
3. When Giorgio felt his toes, he realized they were completely numb.
4. Tanya thought she was funny, but she was actually sarcastic.
5. Calling quickly for professional help is almost always a levelheaded thing to do in an emergency.
6. Olivia was just barely able to identify two shapes in the darkness.
7. Pluto is at the outermost reaches of our solar system.
8. Early in the trip, they decided to change their destination.
9. They crossed a wide expanse of desert.
10. After knocking on the wrong door, Buford turned red with embarrassment.

Practice and Reinforcement (6)
Denotation and Connotation

1. marched
2. wailed
3. munched
4. said
5. rare

Exercise B

1. NU, looked into; NG, snooped
2. NU, asked; NG, whined
3. P, fashionable; NG, trendy
4. NG, decrepit; NU, old
5. NG, tasteless; NU bland
6. NU or P, colorful; NG, gaudy
7. NG, naive; P or NU, innocent
8. P or NU, laughed; NG, snorted
9. P or NU, smart; P, brilliant
10. NU, tired; NG, exhausted

Practice and Reinforcement (7)
Jargon and Gobbledygook

Exercise A

(The wording of answers will vary. Sample responses are given.)

1. a set of data arranged in ascending or descending sequence, depending on a specific key within the data
2. a stringboard or a string course; that is, a horizontal decorative band on a façade
3. a cord that is plucked, struck, or bowed to produce tones when it is stretched across the sounding board of an instrument
4. a group of players that make up a ranked team within a team; for example, a *second string*

Exercise B

(Answers will vary. Possible responses are given.)

1. A penny saved is a penny earned.
2. It is better to give than to receive.
3. A cat has nine lives.
4. Easy come, easy go.
5. An apple a day keeps the doctor away.

Practice and Reinforcement (8)
Mixed Figures of Speech and Clichés

Exercise A

(Answers will vary for each rewrite. Possible responses are given.)

1. Serious problems threatened to engulf her completely.
2. She promised to work hard to shave the fat from the budget.
3. Like a bunch of buzzards, the media sunk its claws into the victim and refused to release him until he talked with them.
4. His climb up the ladder of success was short.

Answer Key

Exercise B

1. The victim appeared to be <u>as dead as a doornail</u>.
   The victim appeared to be dead.

2. <u>At this point in time</u>, the police do not wish to make a statement.
   The police do not wish to make a statement.

3. This case might provide clues to another murder; if so, the police will <u>kill two birds with one stone</u>.
   This case might provide clues to another murder.

4. Police will <u>leave no stone unturned</u> until this case is solved.
   Police will follow up every possible clue and lead until this case is solved.

Chapter Review (Form A)

Exercise A

1. F	6. F
2. T	7. F
3. T	8. F
4. F	9. F
5. T	10. T

Exercise B

(Wording of answers will vary. Sample responses are given.)

1. charivari—a noisy celebration or demonstration; Latin
2. depot—a warehouse or storage facility; French
3. bureau—a desk with drawers; French
4. chintz—brightly colored polished cotton cloth; Hindi
5. cruller—a type of doughnut twisted into a curl; Dutch

Exercise C

1. C	4. J
2. T	5. G
3. MFS	

Chapter Review (Form B)

Exercise A

1. jargon
2. Old English
3. connotations
4. informal English
5. Proto-Indo-European
6. gobbledygook
7. clichés
8. denotation
9. formal English
10. Middle English

a. language appropriate for everyday conversation
b. the dictionary meaning of a word
c. the language family from which English, French, Russian, Latin, Greek, and many other languages are descended
d. language appropriate for serious, dignified occasions
e. the language spoken in England from around 1066 until the late 1400s
f. the special language of a profession or field of activity
g. wordy, puffed-up language
h. the dominant language in England until around 1066
i. the meanings suggested by or associated with a word
j. expressions that are overused or tired

Exercise B

(Answers will vary. Possible responses are given.)

1. Haste makes waste.
2. All that glitters is not gold.

Exercise C

1. T	4. MFS
2. G	5. J
3. C	